Anne Rockwell's
Things
That Go!

CARS
FIRE ENGINES
BIKES

Barnes
&Noble
BOOKS
NEW YORK

D1123652

FIRE ENGINES

I like fire engines.

I like to watch the fire fighters

wash and polish their fire engines.

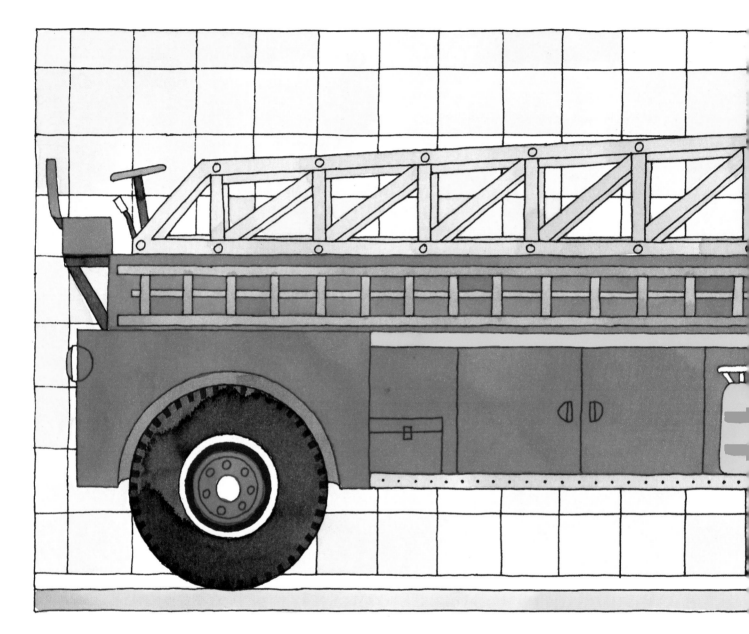

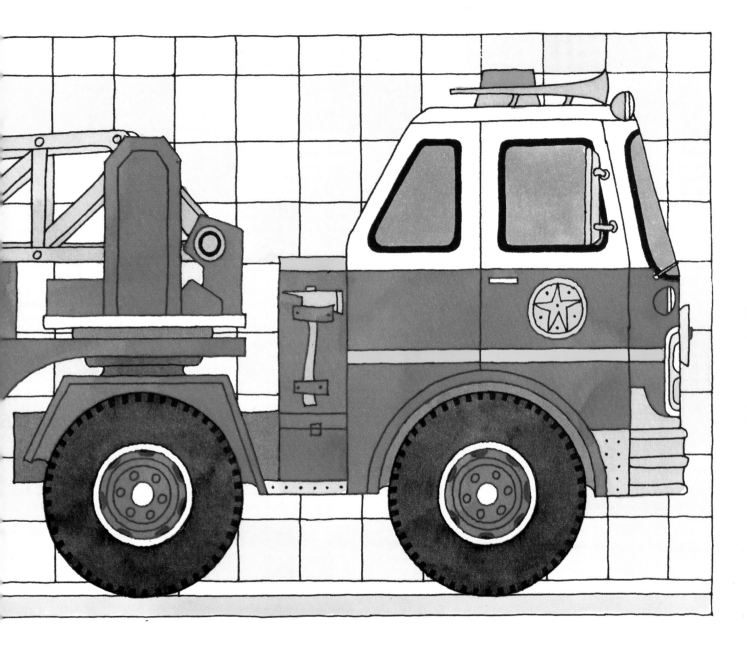

Ladder trucks have long ladders.

Motors raise the ladders high in the air.

Pumper trucks have hoses and pumps.

Water is pumped from a hydrant.

Hoses spray the water on fires.

Some fire engines have pumps

and hoses and ladders.

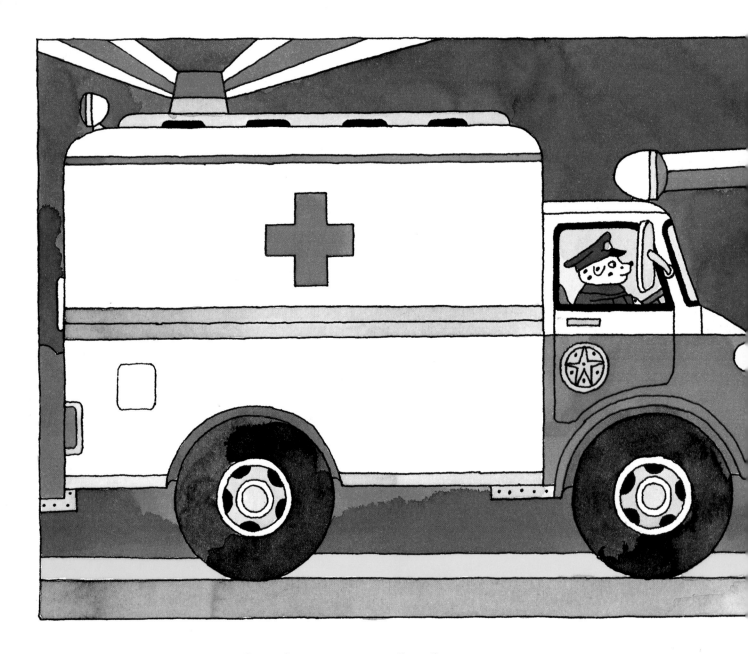

A firehouse ambulance comes
to help anyone who is hurt in a fire.

The fire chief drives a bright red car
and wears a white helmet and coat.

Some fire engines are yellow,

but I like red ones best.

Some fire engines are boats that
put out fires on ships and docks.

They spray water from the harbor.

Fire fighters are brave and strong.

Their fire engines are shiny and beautiful.

I want to be a fire fighter and drive
a real fire engine when I grow up.

BIKES

Little kids ride tricycles.

Big kids ride bicycles with horns that blow.

Parents ride bicycles with seats for babies.

A unicycle is a bike with only one wheel.

A tandem bike has two seats
so friends can ride together.

Racing bikes go very fast.

Delivery bikes in big cities carry food
from stores to homes.

An exercise bike doesn't go anywhere,
but its wheel turns fast.

A motorcycle is a big bike
with a big, noisy motor.

The rider can make it jump over things.

A moped has a little motor.

A motor scooter has two little wheels
and no pedals.

Trail bikes have knobby tires that go
on dirt and through mud puddles.

This cycle has three big, fat tires.
The farmer rides it around the farm.

We ride bikes through city parks.

We ride bikes on country roads.

We ride bikes to school.

Today is my birthday.
Today I got a bicycle with training wheels.

CARS

Cars go everywhere.

They go on six-lane turnpikes

and on dusty, country roads.

They go through dark tunnels

and over airy bridges.

They go fast.

They go slow.

Gasoline makes them go.

There are big cars

and small cars,

old cars

and new cars.

Cars take us far away

and down the street to the store.

Our car is red and shiny.

We get in our car,

and away we go!